Hello Dex		page	3
Unit 1	Discover school	page	7
Halloween		page	19
Unit 2	Discover my body	page	21
Unit 3	Discover my house	page	33
Unit 4	Discover wild animals	page	45
Unit 5	Discover fruit	page	57
Unit 6	Discover jobs	page	69
Unit 7	Discover sports	page	81
Unit 8	Discover daily routines	page	93
Projects		page	105
Picture dictionary		page	121

digital

With digital materials

Including additional Festival lessons (**Halloween, Christmas, Carnival**)

macmillan education

Sandie Mourão

Course consultant: Claire Medwell

Macmillan Education
4 Crinan Street
London N1 9XW
A division of Macmillan Publishers Limited

Companies and representatives throughout the world

Pupil's Book PLUS ISBN 978-0-230-44677-9

Written by Sandie Mourão
The author has asserted her right to be identified as the author of this work in accordance with the Copyright, Designs and Patents Act 1988.

First published 2015

Designed by Carolyn Gibson
Original design by Anthony Godber
Page make-up by Carolyn Gibson
Illustrated by Pablo Gallego (Beehive Illustration)
Additional artwork provided by Tamara Joubert, Daniel Limón, Alek Sotirovski (Beehive Illustration)
Cover design by Macmillan Publishers Limited and Astwood Design Consultancy
Cover illustration by Pablo Gallego (Beehive Illustration)
Picture research by Emily Taylor

Author's acknowledgements:
Many thanks to everyone in the Macmillan team. Special thanks to Claire Medwell.

The publishers would like to thank:
Almudena González Siles, CEIP Benimaclet, Valencia; Ana María Pérez López, CEIP José Iturzaeta, Rivas-Vaciamadrid, Madrid; Asunción Morcillo Escudero, CEIP Leonardo Torres Quevedo, Coslada, Madrid; Isabel Melcón Pérez, Colegio La Purísima, Madrid; Julie Louise Hickin, Col·legi Agora, Sant Cugat del Vallès, Barcelona; Laura López Pérez, CEIP Henares, Mejorada del Campo, Madrid; Miriam Vaquer Wirth, Col·legi Sant Francesc de Assìs, Manacor, Baleares; Yolanda Neira Gómez, CRA Boqueixon-Vedra, Boqueixon, A Coruña.

Printed and bound in Brazil

2022
17

The authors and publishers would like to thank the following for permission to reproduce their photographs:

Alamy/Angela Hampton Picture Library p73(l), Alamy/Horizons WWP p49(tl); **BananaStock** p25(bl); **Corbis**/Tony Latham p97(bl); **Getty Images**/Blend Images p97(tl), Getty Images/Creatas p97(tr), Getty Images/Dorling Kindersley p61(tr), Getty Images/Hero Images p25(r), Getty Images/Indeed p73(r), Getty Images/OJO Images RF p61(br), Getty Images/Brooke Slezak pp13, 27, 39, 51, 63, 75, 87, 97, Getty Images/Vetta pp28, 24, 36, 48, 60, 72, 84, 96; **Image Source** p25(tl); **ThinkStock**/Comstock Images p49(tr), ThinkStock/Getty Images/Hemera p61(tl), ThinkStock/Getty Images/iStockphoto pp49(bl), 97(br), ThinkStock/Getty Images/Tom Le Goff p25(cl).

Commissioned photographs by **Fergus Burnett** pp11(1-6), 18(tl, tr, bl, br), 32,44, 56, 68, 80, 92, 284, 285, 287, 289, 111, 113, 115, 117, 119(tl, tr, bl, br), 37 (tl, tr, bl), 85(tl, bl).

The authors and publishers wish to thank the following for their help with the photoshoot: Rascals Softplay.

Hello Dex
Vocabulary lesson

Hello Dex

Name: ______________________________

1: Vocabulary lesson

Pupil's Book worksheet *page 3*

CD1 12 **Colours song**

Ooh, ooh! I can say the colours
Sing with me
Red and orange, yellow and green
Sing with me

I can say the colours
Sing with me
Blue and pink, purple and brown
Sing with me

I can say the colours
Sing with me
Black and white
Ooh, ooh! I can say the colours
That's right!

- Point to the characters and say their names.
- Trace Dex.
- Colour his spikes.
- Say the colours.
- Sing *Colours* and point to the colours.

digital **Teacher's Presentation Kit for Starter Unit**

Personalisation Discover for yourself

Extra activity Draw and colour Dex. Show his spots and his spikes.

Hello Dex

Vocabulary lesson

1 2 3 4 5

6 7 8 9 10

Hello Dex

Name: ______________________________

2: Vocabulary lesson

Pupil's Book worksheet *page 5*

CD1 13 **Numbers song**

Let's count!
1, 2, 3, 4, 5
Let's count!
6, 7, 8, 9, 10
Let's count!

Let's do it again!

Let's count!
1, 2, 3, 4, 5
Let's count!
6, 7, 8, 9, 10
Let's count!

1, 2, 3, 4, 5, 6, 7, 8, 9, 10

- Find and circle the balls in the picture.
- Count the balls and say the numbers.
- Trace the numbers.
- Match each traced number to one of the balls in the picture.
- Sing *Numbers* and point to the numbers.

Personalisation Discover for yourself

Extra activity Draw a picture of both your hands. How many fingers have you got?

1 Discover school
Vocabulary lesson

1 Discover school

Name: ______________________________

1: Vocabulary lesson

Pupil's Book worksheet *page 7*

CD1 16 CD1 17 **In My School song**

There's a classroom in my school
And a playground too
A classroom and a playground
In my school, in my school, in my school

There's a dining room in my school
And a toilet too
A dining room and a toilet
In my school, in my school, in my school

There's a gym in my school
And a library too
A gym and a library
In my school, in my school, in my school

- Point to the places and say the words.
- Colour each picture frame a different colour and say the colours.
- Match Dex to the place he should be in.
- Colour Dex's frame to match the place.
- Sing *In My School* and point to the places.

digital **Teacher's Presentation Kit for Unit 1**

Personalisation Discover for yourself

Extra activity Draw and colour your classroom.

1 Discover school

Name: ____________________

2: Story lesson

Pupil's Book worksheet *page 9*

CD1 18 **Where's Dex? story**

- Go to the stickers page. Point to the stickers and say *in* or *under*.
- Stick the stickers in the correct place to show what Meg and Charlie saw in the story.
- Match each object to the room it was in.
- Colour the frame around the place where Dex was hiding.

3: Concepts lesson

Photocopiable worksheet *Teacher's Book page 184*

CD1 19 CD1 20 **Pencils Everywhere song**

Pencils here, pencils there
Pencils, pencils everywhere
In the box, and on the chair
Pencils, pencils everywhere

Pencils here, pencils there
Pencils, pencils everywhere
Under the table
And in my hair!
Pencils, pencils everywhere

Pencils here, pencils there
Pencils, pencils everywhere
In, on and under, everywhere
Pencils, pencils everywhere
Arggh!

- Point to the picture and say whether the pencils are *in*, *on* or *under*.
- Colour the pencils blue for *in*.
- Colour the pencils red for *on*.
- Colour the pencils yellow for *under*.
- Count the pencils and circle the correct number.
- Sing *Pencils Everywhere* and point to the picture.

Dex's values lesson

Playing together

1 2 3 4 5 6

1

Discover school

Name: ______________________________

4: Buddy's sounds lesson

Photocopiable worksheet *Teacher's Book page 185*

CD1 21 **Buddy's Beats rap /p/**

1, 2, 3, say with me
/p/, /p/, /p/
/p/ playground!

1, 2, 3, say with me
/p/, /p/, /p/
/p/ plane!

1, 2, 3, say with me
/p/, /p/, /p/
/p/ pencil!

1, 2, 3, say with me
/p/, /p/, /p/
/p/ potatoes!

- Trace the letter /p/.
- Say the sound.
- Point to the pictures and say the words.
- Colour the words beginning with /p/.
- Circle the number of words you find beginning with /p/.
- Say *Buddy's Beats* and point to the words beginning with /p/.

5: Dex's values lesson: Playing together

Pupil's Book worksheet *page 11*

- Point and say *playing together* or *not playing together*.
- Colour the *playing together* frames green and the *not playing together* frames orange.
- Count the photos that show *playing together* and circle the correct number.

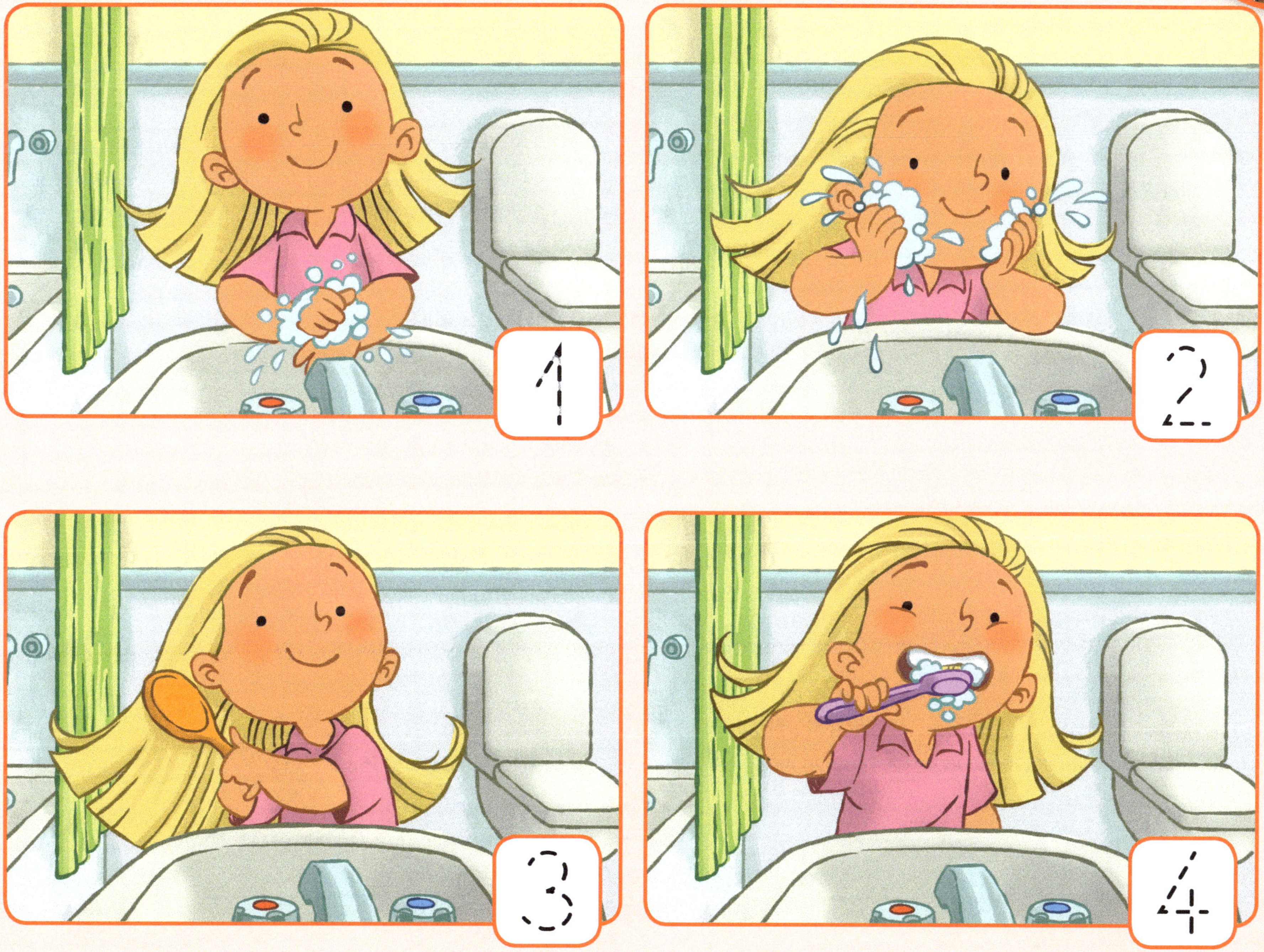
1
2
3
4

1 Discover school

Name: ______________________________

6: Kid's culture lesson

Pupil's Book worksheet *page 13*

CD1 22 CD1 23 **This Is The Way I Wash My Hands nursery rhyme**

This is the way I wash my hands
Wash my hands, wash my hands
This is the way I wash my hands
1, 2, 3!

This is the way I wash my face
Wash my face, wash my face
This is the way I wash my face
1, 2, 3!

This is the way I brush my hair
Brush my hair, brush my hair
This is the way I brush my hair
1, 2, 3!

This is the way I brush my teeth
Brush my teeth, brush my teeth
This is the way I brush my teeth
1, 2, 3!

- Sing *This Is The Way I Wash My Hands* and point to the pictures.
- Trace the numbers illustrating the order of the verses in the nursery rhyme.

7: Speaking and literacy lesson

CD1 18 **Pupils Book worksheet (storybook)** *pages 15–16;* **Photocopiable worksheet** *Teacher's Book page 208*

- Cut out and fold the Pupil's Book pages to make the storybook.
- Cut out and fold the Teacher's Book pages to make the cover.
- Listen to the story and follow the storybook with your finger.

8: Review lesson

CD1 26 **Pupil's Book worksheet** *page 17*

- Listen and circle the correct picture.
- Listen again and check your answer.
- Stick Dex's star in the correct place.

Pupil's Book worksheet *page 18*

- Point to the pictures and say the activities.
- Draw a happy/sad face if you can/can't do the activity.

9: PLUS vocabulary lesson / Extension

Photocopiable worksheet *Teacher's Book page 186*

CD1 28 CD1 29 **In My School PLUS song**

- Point to and say the people.
- Count the people and circle the number for each.
- Colour the picture.
- Sing *In My School PLUS*.

2
PINOCCHIO
THE THREE BEARS

7

4
HEALTHY FOOD
FOOD GUIDE PYRAMID

5

8

1

6

3

Unit 1 review lesson

My learning

1

2

3

My progress review

Name: ____________________

I can …

Teacher: ____________________ Comments: ____________________

Halloween

Lesson 1

Halloween

Name: ______________________________

Lesson 1

Pupil's Book worksheet *page 19*

- Find and say the *pumpkin*, *cat*, *spider* and *skeleton*.
- Circle each item.

digital **Teacher's Resource Centre for Halloween Lesson 2, Christmas lessons and Carnival lessons**

Personalisation Discover for yourself

Extra activity Draw a picture of you in a Halloween costume.

2 Discover my body

Vocabulary lesson

2 Discover my body

Name: ______________________________

1: Vocabulary lesson

Pupil's Book worksheet *page 21*

CD1 31 CD1 32 **Let's March! song**

Let's march!	*Let's march!*	*Let's march!*
Back straight!	*Elbows in!*	*Knees up!*
Let's march!	*Let's march*	*Let's march!*
Back straight!	*Elbows in!*	*Knees up!*
1, 2, 3, 4 (x2)	*1, 2, 3, 4* (x2)	*1, 2, 3, 4* (x2)
Let's march!	*Let's march!*	*Let's march!*
Shoulders down!	*Tummy in!*	*Head straight!*
Let's march!	*Let's march!*	*Let's march!*
Shoulders down!	*Tummy in!*	*Head straight!*
1, 2, 3, 4 (x4)	*1, 2, 3, 4* (x4)	*1, 2, 3, 4* (x5)

- Point to the body parts and say the words.
- Match the body parts to Dex.
- Colour Dex and say the colours.
- Sing *Let's March!* and point to the body parts.

digital **Teacher's Presentation Kit for Unit 2**

Personalisation Discover for yourself

Extra activity Draw a picture of you. Show your elbows, knees, shoulders, head and tummy.

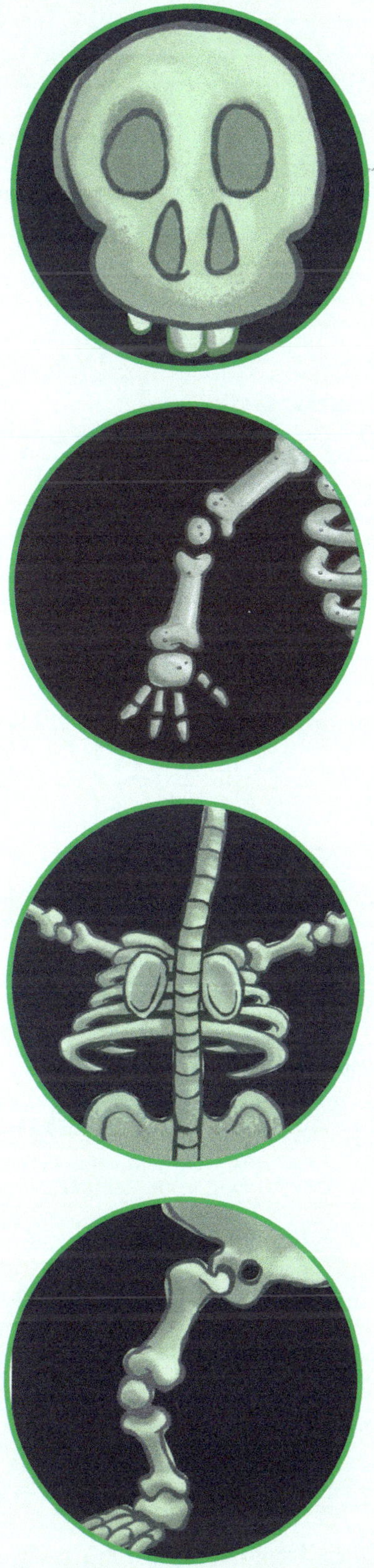

2 Discover my body

Name: ______________________________

2: Story lesson

Pupil's Book worksheet *page 23*

CD1 33 **Ouch, It Hurts! story**

- Point to the body parts and say the words.
- Match the x-rays to Dex's body parts.
- Circle the part of Dex's body which is hurt in the story.
- Complete the face to show Dex's emotion in the story.

3: Concepts lesson

Photocopiable worksheet *Teacher's Book page 187*

CD1 34 CD1 35 **The Shapes song**

It's an oval, an oval
My head is an oval
It's an oval, an oval

It's a diamond, a diamond
My elbow is a diamond
It's a diamond, a diamond

It's a rectangle, a rectangle
My body is a rectangle
It's a rectangle, a rectangle

- Point to and say the shapes.
- Trace.
- Count and circle the number of each shape in the picture.
- Colour each shape a different colour.
- Sing *The Shapes* and point to the shapes.

Going to the doctor

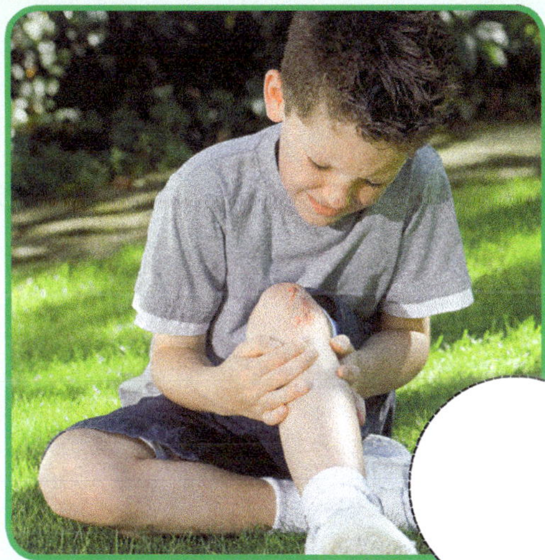

2 Discover my body

Name: ______________________________

4: Buddy's sounds lesson

Photocopiable worksheet *Teacher's Book page 188*

CD1 36 **Buddy's Beats rap /f/**

1, 2, 3, say with me */f/, /f/, /f/* */f/ four!*	*1, 2, 3, say with me* */f/, /f/, /f/* */f/ fast!*
1, 2, 3, say with me */f/, /f/, /f/* */f/ five!*	*1, 2, 3, say with me* */f/, /f/, /f/* */f/ fruit!*

- Trace the letter /f/.
- Say the sound.
- Point to the pictures and say the words.
- Colour the words beginning with /f/.
- Circle the number of words you find beginning with /f/.
- Say *Buddy's Beats* and point to the words beginning with /f/.

5: Dex's values lesson: Going to the doctor

Pupil's Book worksheet *page 25*

- Trace the frame around the doctor.
- Look at the photos and say whether they need to go to the doctor. Match to the photo of the doctor if they do.
- Go to the stickers page. Stick the correct face next to the photos.

1
2
3
4

2 Discover my body

Name: ____________________

6: Kid's culture lesson

Pupil's Book worksheet *page 27*

CD1 37 CD1 38 **One Finger, One Thumb nursery rhyme**

One finger, one thumb, keep moving (x3)
We'll all be happy and play.

One finger, one thumb, one arm, keep moving (x3)
We'll all be happy and play.

One finger, one thumb, one arm, one leg, keep moving (x3)
We'll all be happy and play.

One finger, one thumb, one arm, one leg,
jump up and down, keep moving (x3)
We'll all be happy and play.

- Point to the pictures and say the words.
- Match the actions that appear in the nursery rhyme to the outlines.
- Sing *One Finger, One Thumb* and point to the pictures.

7: Speaking and literacy lesson

CD1 33 **Pupils Book worksheet (storybook)** *pages 29–30;*
Photocopiable worksheet *Teacher's Book page 208*

- Cut out and fold the Pupil's Book pages to make the storybook.
- Cut out and fold the Teacher's Book pages to make the cover.
- Listen to the story and follow the storybook with your finger.

8: Review lesson

CD1 41 **Pupil's Book worksheet** *page 31*

- Listen and circle the correct picture.
- Listen again and check your answer.
- Stick Dex's star in the correct place.

Pupil's Book worksheet *page 32*

- Point to the pictures and say the activities.
- Draw a happy/sad face if you can/can't do the activity.

9: PLUS vocabulary lesson / Extension

Photocopiable worksheet *Teacher's Book page 189*

CD1 43 CD1 44 **Let's March! PLUS song**

- Point to and say the body parts.
- Match the body parts to Meg.
- Colour.
- Sing *Let's March! PLUS.*

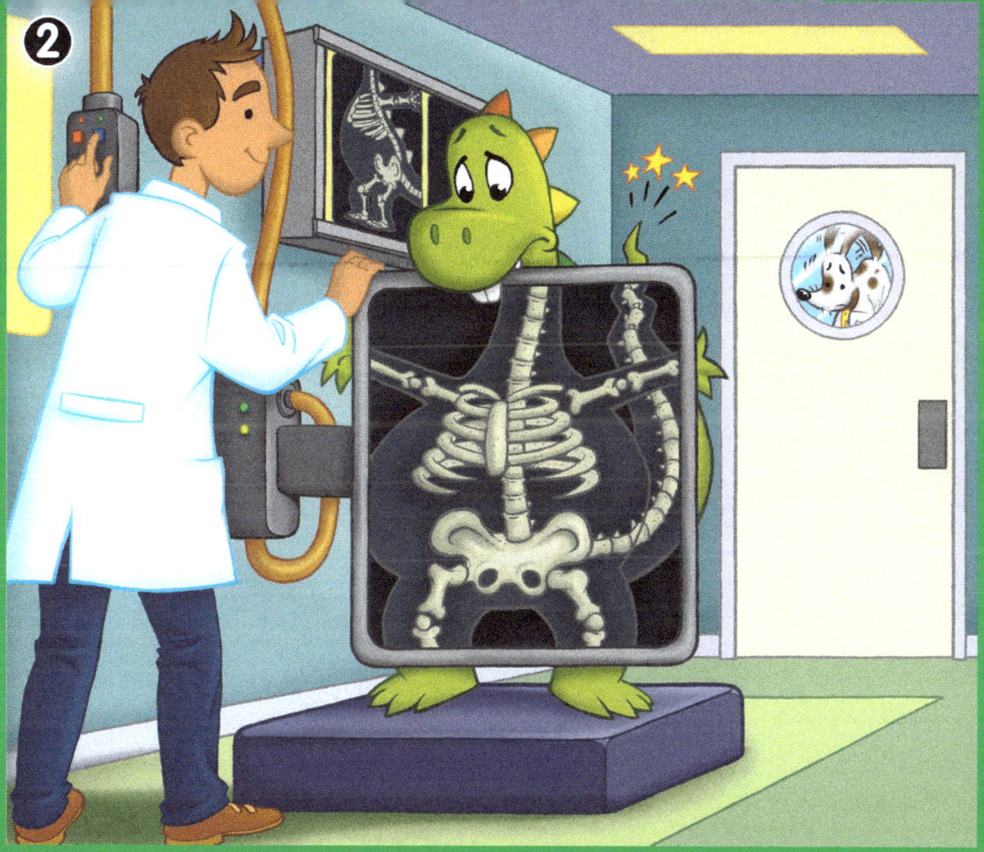
2

7

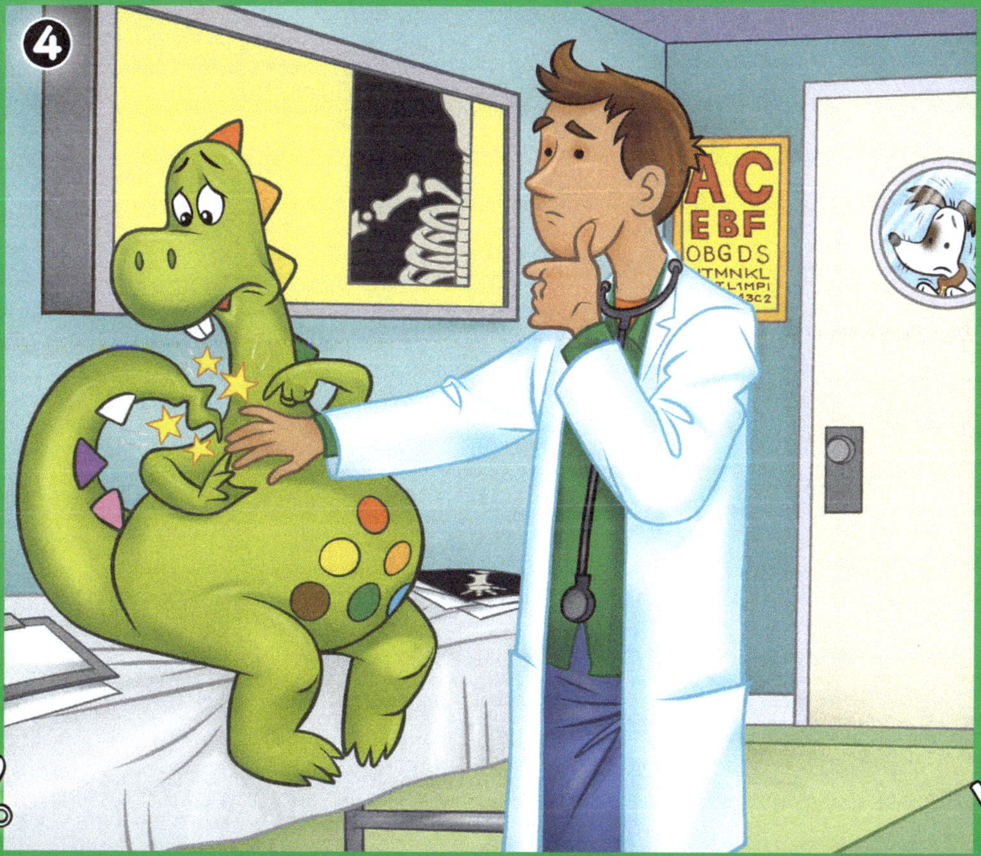
4
AC
EBF
OBGDS

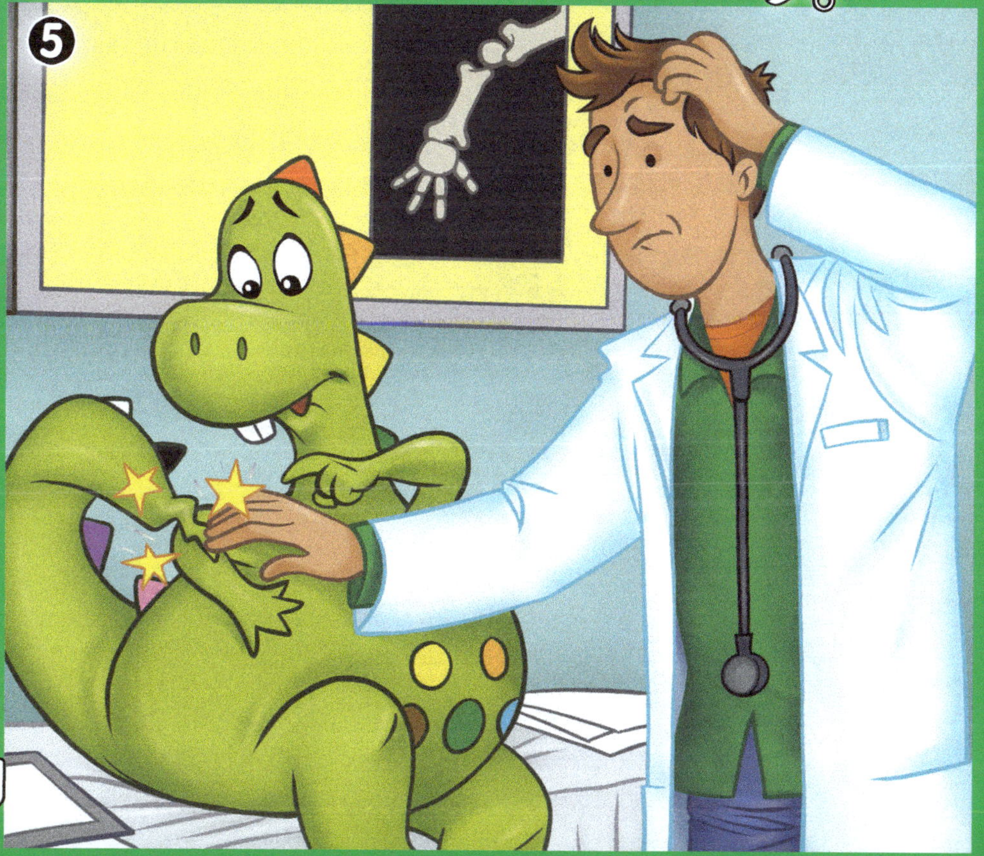
5

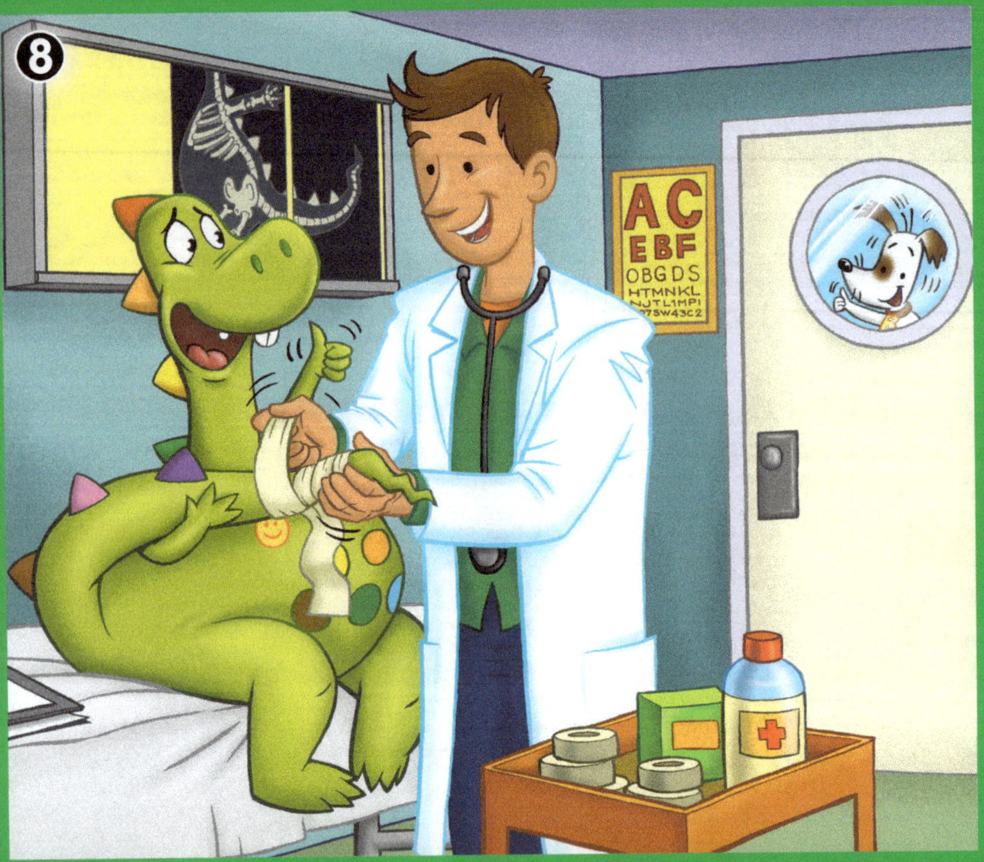
8
AC
EBF
OBGDS

1
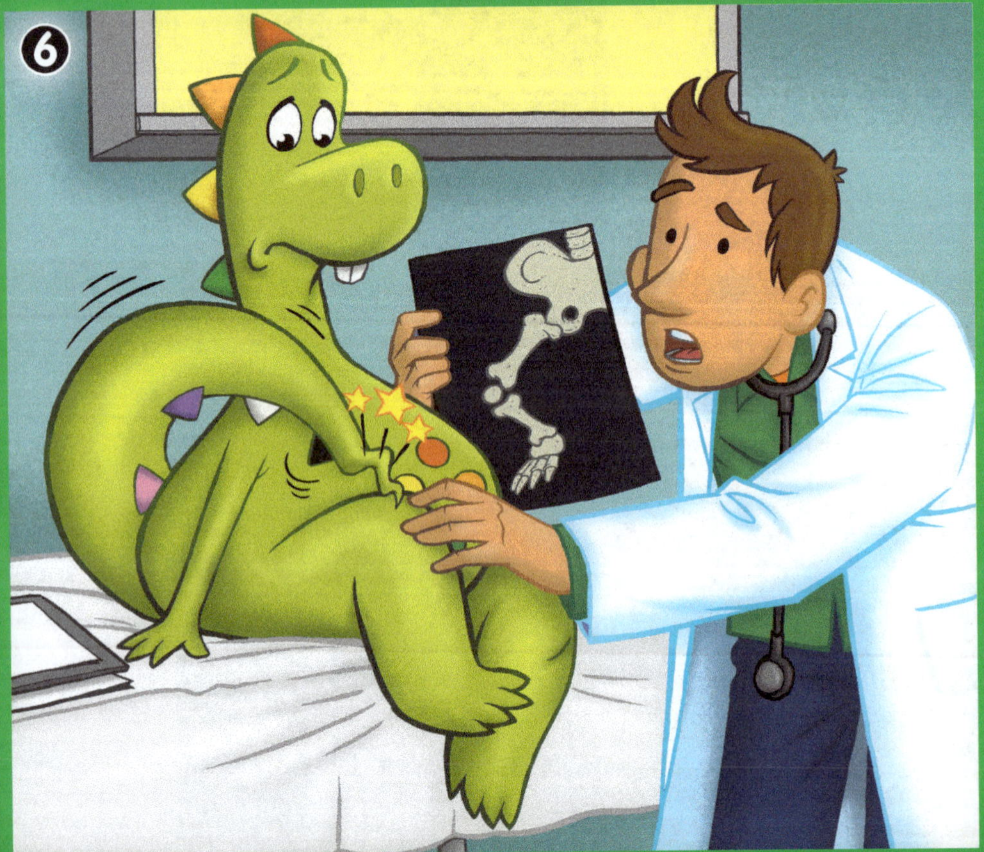
6

3
AC
EBF
OBGDS

Unit 2 review lesson

My learning review

1

2

3

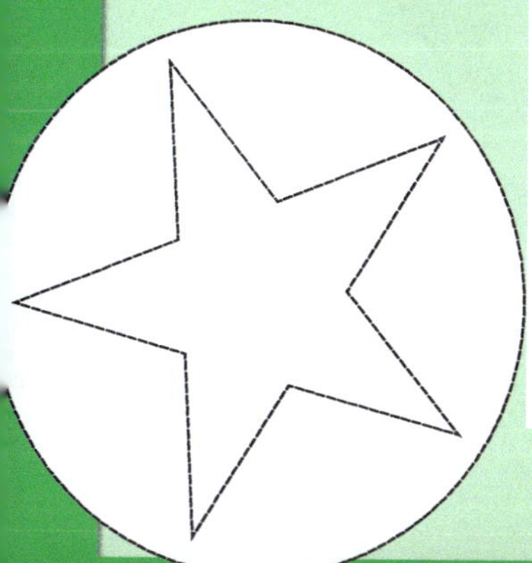

My progress review

Name: ______________________________

I can …

Teacher: ____________________ Comments: ____________________

3 Discover my house

Vocabulary lesson

3 Discover my house

Name: ______________________

1: Vocabulary lesson

Pupil's Book worksheet *page 33*

CD2 2 CD2 3 **In My House song**

There's a living room in my house and a bedroom too
Let's sing in the living room
Let's sing in the bedroom

There's a bathroom in my house and a kitchen too
Let's sing in the bathroom
Let's sing in the kitchen
Let's sing in my house
Let's sing in my house all day
Let's sing in my house all day (x4)

There's a garden in my house and a garage too
Let's sing in the garden
Let's sing in the garage
Let's sing in my house
Let's sing in my house all day
Let's sing in my house all day (x4)

- Point to the pictures and say the places in the house.
- Match the activities to the correct places in the house.
- Draw the missing activity and match it to the correct place in the house.
- Colour each place in the house a different colour and say the colours.
- Sing *In My House* and point to the places.

digital ➡ **Teacher's Presentation Kit for Unit 3**

Personalisation Discover for yourself

Extra activity Draw your bedroom.

1

2

3

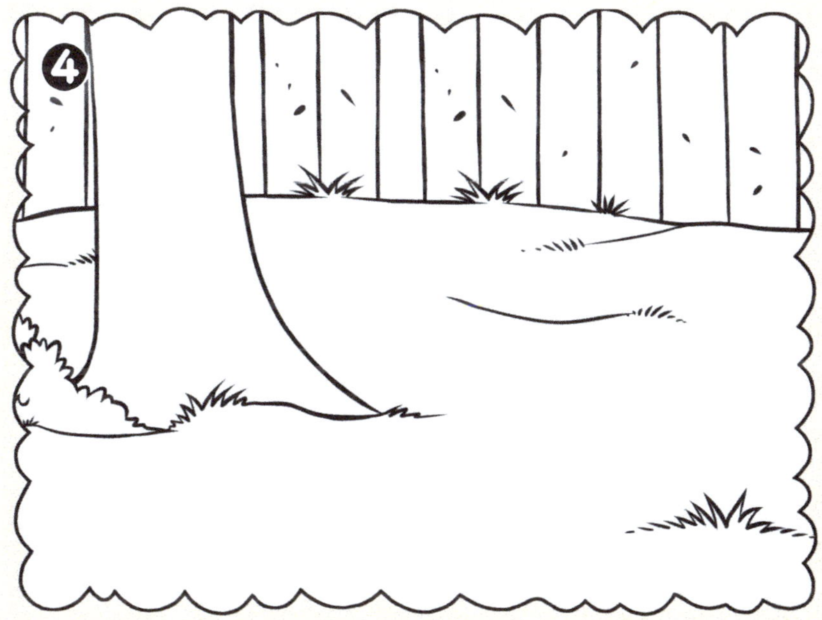
4

3 Discover my house

Name: ______________________________

2: Story lesson

Pupil's Book worksheet *page 35*

CD2 4 **Dex's Dream story**

- Point to the pictures and say the rooms.
- Circle the object in each picture that Dex eats/uses in the story.
- Draw what happens at the end of the story in picture 4.
- Colour picture 4.

Asking for permission

3: Concepts lesson

Photocopiable worksheet *Teacher's Book page 190*

CD2 5 CD2 6 **The Bear song**

I'm a big bear
I'm a big bear
I'm Daddy bear
I'm a big daddy bear

I'm a medium bear
I'm a medium bear
I'm Mummy bear
I'm a medium mummy bear

I'm a small bear
I'm a small bear
I'm Baby bear
I'm a small baby bear

- Point to the bears and clothes and say *small*, *medium* or *big*.
- Match the clothes to the bears.
- Colour the *big* clothes red, the *medium* clothes blue and the *small* clothes green.
- Sing *The Bear* and point to the *small*, *medium* and *big* clothes.

Dex's values lesson

Asking for permission

3 Discover my house

Name: ______________________________

4: Buddy's sounds lesson

Photocopiable worksheet *Teacher's Book page 191*

CD2 7 **Buddy's Beats rap /g/**

1, 2, 3, say with me
/g/, /g/, /g/
/g/ garage!

1, 2, 3, say with me
/g/, /g/, /g/
/g/ granny!

1, 2, 3, say with me
/g/, /g/, /g/
/g/ garden!

1, 2, 3, say with me
/g/, /g/, /g/
/g/ grandad!

- Trace the letter /g/.
- Say the sound.
- Point to the pictures and say the words.
- Colour the words beginning with /g/.
- Circle the number of words you find beginning with /g/.
- Say *Buddy's Beats* and point to the words beginning with /g/.

5: Dex's values lesson: Asking for permission

Pupil's Book worksheet *page 37*

- Point to the photo and say *asking for permission* or *not asking for permission*.
- Colour the frame green if the photo shows *asking for permission*.
- Colour the frame red if the photo shows *not asking for permission*.
- Draw a happy face for *asking for permission* and a sad face for *not asking for permission*.
- Draw a picture of you *asking for permission*, colour the frame green and draw a happy face.

5
4
3
2
1

3 Discover my house

Name: ______________________________

6: Kid's culture lesson

Pupil's Book worksheet *page 39*

CD2 8 CD2 9 **There Are Five In The Bed nursery rhyme**

There are five in the bed
And the little one says
Roll over! Roll over!
So we all roll over and one falls out

There are four in the bed
And the little one says
Roll over! Roll over!
So we all roll over and one falls out

There are three in the bed
And the little one says
Roll over! Roll over!
So we all roll over and one falls out

There are two in the bed
And the little one says
Roll over! Roll over!
So we all roll over and one falls out

There's one in the bed
And the little one says
Goodnight!

- Stick the correct sticker on each picture.
- Count the children in each picture and say the number.
- Trace the numbers.
- Sing *There Are Five In The Bed* and point to the pictures.

7: Speaking and literacy lesson

CD2 4 **Pupils Book worksheet (storybook)** *pages 41–42;*
Photocopiable worksheet *Teacher's Book page 208*

- Cut out and fold the Pupil's Book pages to make the storybook.
- Cut out and fold the Teacher's Book pages to make the cover.
- Listen to the story and follow the storybook with your finger.

8: Review lesson

CD2 12 **Pupil's Book worksheet** *page 43*

- Listen and circle the correct picture.
- Listen again and check your answer.
- Stick Dex's star in the correct place.

Pupil's Book worksheet *page 44*

- Point to the pictures and say the activities.
- Draw a happy/sad face if you can/can't do the activity.

9: PLUS vocabulary lesson / Extension

Photocopiable worksheet *Teacher's Book page 192*

CD2 14 CD2 15 **In My House PLUS song**

- Point to and say the rooms/places.
- Draw and colour a picture of your house or flat.
- Match the pictures to the rooms in your house or flat.
- Sing *In My House PLUS*.

2

7

4

5

8
THE THREE BEARS
B

1
ZZZZ...
3
THE THREE BEARS

6

3

My learning review

1

2

3

My progress review

Name: ____________________

I can ...

Teacher: ____________________

Comments: ____________________

4 Discover wild animals

Vocabulary lesson

4 Discover wild animals

Name: ______________________

1: Vocabulary lesson

Pupil's Book worksheet *page 45*

CD2 17 CD2 18 **I Can See A Lion song**

I can see a lion! *Where's the lion?* *Over there!*	*I can see a zebra!* *Where's the zebra?* *Over there! Over there!*
I can see a monkey! *Where's the monkey?* *Over there! Over there!*	*I can see a giraffe!* *Where's the giraffe?* *Over there!*
I can see an elephant! *Where's the elephant?* *Over there!*	*I can see a hippo!* *Where's the hippo?* *Over there! Over there!*

- Point to the animals in the picture and say the words.
- Count the animals in the picture and write the number.
- Which animal is missing? Draw the missing lion in the picture.
- Colour each animal a different colour and say the colour.
- Sing *I Can See A Lion* and point to the animals.

digital **Teacher's Presentation Kit for Unit 4**

Personalisation Discover for yourself

Extra activity Draw your favourite wild animal.

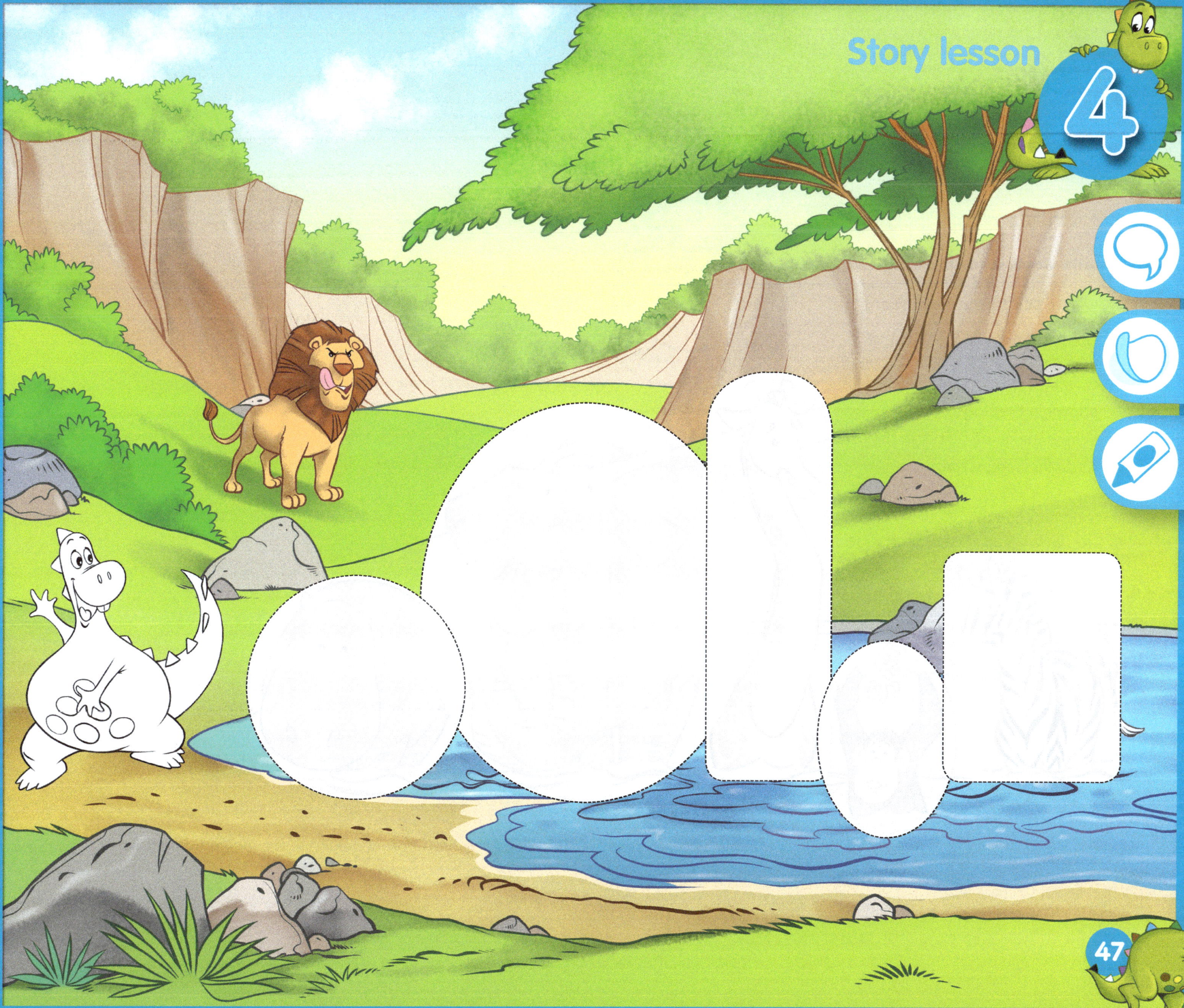

4 Discover wild animals

Name: ______________________

2: Story lesson

Pupil's Book worksheet *page 47*

CD2 19 **At The Safari Park story**

- Go to the sticker page. Point to the animals and say the words.
- Stick the animals in the order they appear in the story.
- Who is the hero? Colour in the hero, Dex.
- Circle the hungry lion.

3: Concepts lesson

Photocopiable worksheet *Teacher's Book page 193*

CD2 20 CD2 21 **Long And Short song**

Long, long, long!
An elephant's trunk
Is long
Short, short, short!
An elephant's tail
Is short
Long, short (x2)

Long, long, long!
A giraffe's neck
Is long
Short, short, short!
A giraffe's tail
Is short
Long, short (x2)

- Point to and say the animals.
- Draw the missing *long* and *short* body parts.
- Colour the frame yellow if the animal's body part is *long*.
- Colour the frame green if the animal's body part is *short*.
- Colour the animals.
- Sing *Long And Short* and point to the *long* and *short* body parts.

Dex's values lesson

Looking after animals

4 Discover wild animals

Name: ______________________________

4: Buddy's sounds lesson

Photocopiable worksheet *Teacher's Book page 194*

CD2 22 **Buddy's Beats rap /l/**

1, 2, 3, say with me
/l/, /l/, /l/
/l/ library!

1, 2, 3, say with me
/l/, /l/, /l/
/l/ lion!

1, 2, 3, say with me
/l/, /l/, /l/
/l/ living room!

1, 2, 3, say with me
/l/, /l/, /l/
/l/ long!

- Trace the letter /l/.
- Say the sound.
- Point to the pictures and say the words.
- Colour the words beginning with /l/.
- Circle the number of words you find beginning with /l/.
- Say *Buddy's Beats* and point to the words beginning with /l/.

5: Dex's values lesson: Looking after animals

Pupil's Book worksheet *page 49*

- Point and say *looking after animals* or *not looking after animals*.
- Draw a tick if the photo shows a happy animal being looked after.
- Draw a cross if the photo shows a sad animal not being looked after.
- Draw the elephant being looked after in the blank box.

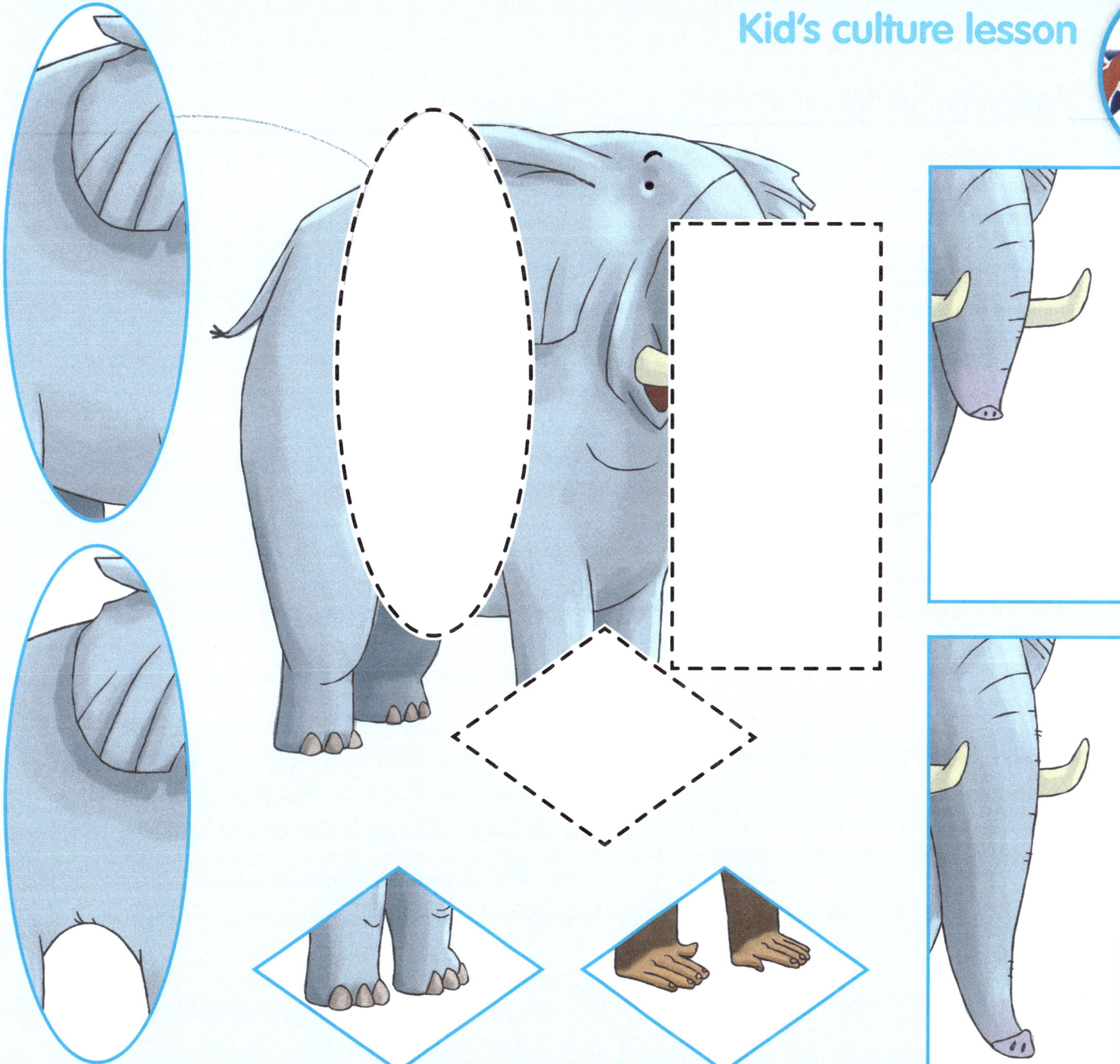

4 Discover wild animals

Name: ______________________

6: Kid's culture lesson

Pupil's Book worksheet *page 51*

CD2 23 CD2 24 **An Elephant Walks Like This And That nursery rhyme**

An elephant walks like this and that
He's very big and very fat
He has no fingers and he has no toes
But goodness gracious, what a long nose!

- Point to the shapes and say the words.
- Trace the shapes.
- Match the correct shapes to the picture.
- Draw the missing parts of the picture within the shapes.
- Sing *An Elephant Walks Like This And That* and point to the picture.

7: Speaking and literacy lesson

CD2 19 **Pupils Book worksheet (storybook)** *pages 53–54;*
Photocopiable worksheet *Teacher's Book page 208*

- Cut out and fold the Pupil's Book pages to make the storybook.
- Cut out and fold the Teacher's Book pages to make the cover.
- Listen to the story and follow the storybook with your finger.

8: Review lesson

CD2 27 **Pupil's Book worksheet** *page 55*

- Listen and circle the correct picture.
- Listen again and check your answer.
- Stick Dex's star in the correct place.

Pupil's Book worksheet *page 56*

- Point to the pictures and say the activities.
- Draw a happy/sad face if you can/can't do the activity.

9: PLUS vocabulary lesson / Extension

Photocopiable worksheet *Teacher's Book page 195*

CD2 29 CD2 30 **I Can See A Lion PLUS song**

- Point to and say the names of the animals.
- Trace the heads of the animals.
- Colour each animal a different colour.
- Cut out the animals and glue them in the correct order.
- Sing *I Can See A Lion PLUS*.

2

7

4

5

8

1

6

3

1

2

3

My progress review

Name: ______________________

I can …

Teacher: ______________________ Comments: ______________________

5 Discover fruit

Vocabulary lesson

5 Discover fruit

Name: ______________________________

1: Vocabulary lesson

Pupil's Book worksheet *page 57*

CD2 32 CD2 33 **The Fruit song**

Bananas, bananas
Yellow bananas
I like bananas
I do too!

Pears, pears
Green pears
I like pears
I do too!

Plums, plums
Purple plums
I like plums
I do too!

Cherries, cherries
Red cherries
I like cherries
I do too!

Oranges, oranges
Big oranges
I like oranges
I do too!

Apples, apples
Red apples
I like apples
I do too!

- Find the fruit in the picture and say the words.
- Colour each fruit the correct colour and say the colours.
- Sing *The Fruit* and point to the fruit.

digital **Teacher's Presentation Kit for Unit 5**

Personalisation Discover for yourself

Extra activity Draw your favourite fruit.

Story lesson 5

3

3

4

6

8

10

5 Discover fruit

Name: ______________________________

2: Story lesson

Pupil's Book worksheet *page 59*

CD2 34 **A Big Fruit Salad story**

- Go to the sticker sheet. Point to the fruit and say the words.
- Stick the stickers in the correct place.
- Trace the number of each fruit the children pick in the story.
- Trace the bowl.
- Draw and colour a fruit salad in the bowl.

3: Concepts lesson

Photocopiable worksheet *Teacher's Book page 196*

CD2 35 CD2 36 **High And Low song**

High, high, high
I can go high
Low, low, low
I can go low

High, high, high
Low, low, low
I can go high
And I can go low

- Point to the picture and say the fruit.
- Say whether the fruit is *high* or *low*.
- Colour the *high* boxes orange and the *low* boxes purple.
- Colour the boxes of fruit below the picture to match.
- Sing *High And Low* and point to the high and low fruit.

Helping

5 Discover fruit

Name: ______________________________

4: Buddy's sounds lesson

Photocopiable worksheet *Teacher's Book page 197*

CD2 37 **Buddy's Beats rap /b/**

1, 2, 3, say with me
/b/, /b/, /b/
/b/ bathroom!

1, 2, 3, say with me
/b/, /b/, /b/
/b/ banana!

1, 2, 3, say with me
/b/, /b/, /b/
/b/ bedroom!

- Trace the letter /b/.
- Say the sound.
- Point to the pictures and say the words.
- Colour the words beginning with /b/.
- Circle the number of words you find beginning with /b/.
- Say *Buddy's Beats* and point to the words beginning with /b/.

5: Dex's values lesson: Helping

Pupil's Book worksheet *page 61*

- Point to each photo and say if the person needs some help.
- Colour the frame orange if the photo shows a person who needs some help.
- Colour the frame blue if the photo shows a person who doesn't need some help.
- Draw a picture of you in the frame.
- Can you help each person? Match the picture of you to the people you can help.

1 2 3 4 5 6 7 8 9 10

1 2 3 4 5 6 7 8 9 10

5 Discover fruit

Name: ______________________

6: Kid's culture lesson

Pupil's Book worksheet *page 63*

CD2 38 CD2 39 **One Banana, Two Bananas nursery rhyme**

One banana, two bananas, three bananas, four!
Five bananas, six bananas, seven bananas, more!

- Find and circle the seven differences in the second picture.
- Say the differences.
- Count and circle the number of bananas in each picture.
- Sing *One Banana, Two Bananas* and point to the bananas.

Seven differences:
1 orange and white tent 2 six balloons 3 five bananas
4 bowl of cherries 5 toffee apple 6 monkey
7 the clown's trousers

7: Speaking and literacy lesson

CD2 34 **Pupils Book worksheet (storybook)** *pages 65–66;*
Photocopiable worksheet *Teacher's Book page 208*

- Cut out and fold the Pupil's Book pages to make the storybook.
- Cut out and fold the Teacher's Book pages to make the cover.
- Listen to the story and follow the storybook with your finger.

8: Review lesson

CD2 42 **Pupil's Book worksheet** *page 67*

- Listen and circle the correct picture.
- Listen again and check your answer.
- Stick Dex's star in the correct place.

Pupil's Book worksheet *page 68*

- Point to the pictures and say the activities.
- Draw a happy/sad face if you can/can't do the activity.

9: PLUS vocabulary lesson / Extension

Photocopiable worksheet *Teacher's Book page 198*

CD2 44 CD2 45 **The Fruit PLUS song**

- Point to and say the fruit.
- Draw the missing fruit to complete each sequence.
- Colour each fruit a different colour.
- Sing *The Fruit PLUS*.

2

7

4

5

8

1

6

3

My learning review

1

2

3

My progress review

Name: ____________________

I can …

Teacher: ____________________ Comments: ____________________

6 Discover jobs

Vocabulary lesson

6 Discover jobs

Name: ____________________

1: Vocabulary lesson

Pupil's Book worksheet *page 69*

CD3 2 CD3 3 **I Want To Be A Fire Fighter song**

I want to be a fire fighter!
I want to be a teacher!
Fire fighter! Teacher!
Yes, yes, I do

I want to be a police officer
I want to be a mechanic
Police officer! Mechanic!
Yes, yes, I do

I want to be a waiter
I want to be a hairdresser
Waiter! Hairdresser!
Yes, yes, I do

- Point to the pictures and say the jobs.
- Match the bodies to the legs.
- Sing *I Want To Be A Fire Fighter* and point to the jobs.

digital **Teacher's Presentation Kit for Unit 6**

Personalisation Discover for yourself

Extra activity What do you want to be? Draw a picture of the job you like.

6 Discover jobs

Name: ______________________________

2: Story lesson

Pupil's Book worksheet *page 71*

CD3 4 **What's Your Job? story**

- Go to the sticker page. Stick the stickers on the correct family member.
- Point to the people and say the jobs.
- Colour Dex.

3: Concepts lesson

Photocopiable worksheet *Teacher's Book page 199*

CD3 5 CD3 6 **Heavy And Light song**

Heavy, heavy
An elephant is heavy
It's heavy!

Light, light
A pencil is light
It's light!

- Point to the pictures and say the words.
- Point again and say *light* or *heavy*.
- Draw the objects in the correct frame for *light* or *heavy*.
- Draw another light or heavy object in each frame.
- Colour the *heavy* objects red and the *light* objects yellow.
- Sing *Heavy And Light* and point to the light and heavy objects.

STOP

6

Discover jobs

Name: ______________________________

4: Buddy's sounds lesson

Photocopiable worksheet *Teacher's Book page 200*

CD3 7 **Buddy's Beats rap /w/**

1, 2, 3, say with me
/w/, /w/, /w/
/w/ waiter!

1, 2, 3, say with me
/w/, /w/, /w/
/w/ water!

1, 2, 3, say with me
/w/, /w/, /w/
/w/ white!

- Trace the letter /w/.
- Say the sound.
- Point to the pictures and say the words.
- Colour the words beginning with /w/.
- Circle the number of words you find beginning with /w/.
- Say *Buddy's Beats* and point to the words beginning with /w/.

5: Dex's values lesson: Road safety

Pupil's Book worksheet *page 73*

- Point and say whether the photos show *stopping and waiting* or *crossing*.
- Colour the traffic lights. Use green to show *crossing* and red to show *stopping and waiting*.
- Trace the borders.

1

2

6 Discover jobs

Name: ____________________

6: Kid's culture lesson

Pupil's Book worksheet *page 75*

CD3 8 CD3 9 **The Farmer's In His House nursery rhyme**

The farmer's in his house
The farmer's in his house
Hey ho, hey ho!
The farmer's in his house

The farmer's got a wife
The farmer's got a wife
Hey ho, hey ho!
The farmer's got a wife

The wife's got a baby
The wife's got a baby
Hey ho, hey ho!
The wife's got a baby

The baby's got a dog
The baby's got a dog
Hey ho, hey ho!
The baby's got a dog

We all pat the dog
We all pat the dog
Hey ho, hey ho!
We all pat the dog

- Find and circle ten differences in the second picture.
- Say the differences.
- Trace the tick for the picture that illustrates the nursery rhyme.
- Sing *The Farmer's In His House* and point to the picture.

Ten differences:
1 policeman hat 2 frowning wife 3 green shirt
4 brown bucket 5 apples 6 yellow circle
7 cat 8 teddy bear 9 six chicks 10 small cake

7: Speaking and literacy lesson

CD3 4 **Pupils Book worksheet (storybook)** *pages 77–78;*
Photocopiable worksheet *Teacher's Book page 208*

- Cut out and fold the Pupil's Book pages to make the storybook.
- Cut out and fold the Teacher's Book pages to make the cover.
- Listen to the story and follow the storybook with your finger.

8: Review lesson

CD3 12 **Pupil's Book worksheet** *page 79*

- Listen and circle the correct picture.
- Listen again and check your answer.
- Stick Dex's star in the correct place.

Pupil's Book worksheet *page 80*

- Point to the pictures and say the activities.
- Draw a happy/sad face if you can/can't do the activity.

9: PLUS vocabulary lesson / Extension

Photocopiable worksheet *Teacher's Book page 201*

CD3 14 CD3 15 **I Want To Be A Fire Fighter PLUS song**

- Point to and say the jobs.
- Trace and match the children to the jobs.
- Draw yourself and the job that you would like to do.
- Sing *I Want To Be A Fire Fighter PLUS.*

2
Oil

7

4

5

8

1
Service

6

3
POLICE
STOP

1

2

3

My progress review

Name: ______________________

I can …

Teacher: ______________________ Comments: ______________________

7 Discover sports

Vocabulary lesson

1 2 3 4 5 6 7 8 9 10

7 Discover sports

Name: ______________________________

1: Vocabulary lesson

Pupil's Book worksheet *page 81*

CD3 17 CD3 18 **I Like Running song**

I like running
I like running
I like running with my friends

I like swimming
I like swimming
I like swimming with my friends

I like playing football
I like playing football
I like playing football with my friends

I like skating
I like skating
I like skating with my friends

I like riding a bike
I like riding a bike
I like riding a bike with my friends

I like playing basketball
I like playing basketball
I like playing basketball with my friends

- Point to the sports and say the words.
- Count the number of children playing each sport in the big picture and write the number in the blank boxes.
- Sing *I Like Running* and point to the sports.

digital **Teacher's Presentation Kit for Unit 7**

Personalisation Discover for yourself

Extra activity Draw your favourite sport.

7 Discover sports

Name: ______________________

2: Story lesson

Pupil's Book worksheet *page 83*

CD3 19 **I Like Sport story**

- Go to the sticker page. Point to the pictures and say the sports.
- Stick the stickers on the page in the order you hear them in the story.
- Match Dex to the sports he's good at in the story.
- Trace the basketball.
- Colour the basketball and say the colour.

Not giving up

3: Concepts lesson

Photocopiable worksheet *Teacher's Book page 202*

CD3 20 CD3 21 **Me And You song**

One, two, me and you
I'm in front of you
One, two, me and you
I'm behind you

One, two, me and you
I'm in front of you
One, two, me and you
I'm behind you

- Point to the pictures and say *in front of* or *behind*.
- Colour the frames green for *in front of*.
- Colour the frames blue for *behind*.
- Sing *Me And You* and point to the pictures.

Dex's values lesson

Trying

7 Discover sports

Name: ______________________

4: Buddy's sounds lesson

Photocopiable worksheet *Teacher's Book page 203*

CD3 22 **Buddy's Beats rap /s/**

1, 2, 3, say with me
/s/, /s/, /s/
/s/ swimming!

1, 2, 3, say with me
/s/, /s/, /s/
/s/ six!

1, 2, 3, say with me
/s/, /s/, /s/
/s/ seven!

- Trace the letter /s/.
- Say the sound.
- Point to the pictures and say the words.
- Colour the words beginning with /s/.
- Say *Buddy's Beats* and point to the words beginning with /s/.
- Draw the missing item from *Buddy's Beats*.
- Circle the total number of words beginning with /s/.

5: Dex's values lesson: Trying

Pupil's Book worksheet *page 85*

- Point and say *trying* or *not trying*.
- Draw a happy face for the photo that shows *trying*.
- Draw a sad face for the photo that shows *not trying*.
- Draw a picture that shows *trying* and draw a happy face.
- Draw a picture that shows *not trying* and draw a sad face.
- Colour the frames green for the photos/drawings that show *trying*.
- Colour the frames red for the photos/drawings that show *giving up*.

Kid's culture lesson

1 2 3 4 5 6 7 8 9 10

7 Discover sports

Name: ______________________________

6: Kid's culture lesson

Pupil's Book worksheet *page 87*

CD3 23 CD3 24 **Wee Willie Winkie nursery rhyme**

Wee Willie Winkie
Running through the town
Upstairs and downstairs
In his dressing gown

Knocking at the windows
Calling through the lock
'Are the children all in bed?
It's almost eight o'clock'

- Trace the path of Wee Willie Winkie through the town.
- Count and circle the total number of children in the four houses.
- Draw the total number of children in the bed.
- Write the number on the bed.
- Sing *Wee Willie Winkie* and point to the picture.

7: Speaking and literacy lesson

CD3 19 **Pupils Book worksheet (storybook)** *pages 89–90;*
Photocopiable worksheet *Teacher's Book page 208*

- Cut out and fold the Pupil's Book pages to make the storybook.
- Cut out and fold the Teacher's Book pages to make the cover.
- Listen to the story and follow the storybook with your finger.

8: Review lesson

CD3 27 **Pupil's Book worksheet** *page 91*

- Listen and circle the correct picture.
- Listen again and check your answer.
- Stick Dex's star in the correct place.

Pupil's Book worksheet *page 92*

- Point to the pictures and say the activities.
- Draw a happy/sad face if you can/can't do the activity.

9: PLUS vocabulary lesson / Extension

Photocopiable worksheet *Teacher's Book page 204*

CD3 29 CD3 30 **I Like Running PLUS song**

- Point to and say the sport Dex is doing.
- Match each sport to the correct equipment.
- Colour each sport and say the colours.
- Sing *I Like Running PLUS*.

2
FINISH

7
7
2

4

5

8

1

6

3

1

2

3

My progress review

Name: ______________________

I can …

Teacher: ______________________ Comments: ______________________

8 Discover daily routines

Vocabulary lesson

1 2 3 4 5 6

8 Discover daily routines

Name: ______________________

1: Vocabulary lesson

Pupil's Book worksheet *page 93*

CD3 32 CD3 33 **My Day Is Fun song**

My day is fun, fun, fun
Fun, fun, fun
I get up, I get dressed
I get up, I get dressed
My day is fun

My day is fun, fun, fun
Fun, fun, fun
I have breakfast, I have dinner
I have breakfast, I have dinner
My day is fun

My day is fun, fun, fun
Fun, fun, fun
I have a bath, I go to bed
I have a bath, I go to bed
My day is fun

My day is fun, fun, fun
My day is fun

- Point to the pictures and say the words.
- Draw arrows between the pictures to show the sequence, from morning to night.
- Number the activities in the correct order, from morning to night.
- Colour the pictures.
- Sing *My Day Is Fun* and point to the pictures.

digital **Teacher's Presentation Kit for Unit 8**

Personalisation Discover for yourself

Extra activity: Draw a picture of you doing your favourite daily routine.

1

2

3

4

8 Discover daily routines

Name: ____________________

2: Story lesson

Pupil's Book worksheet *page 95*

CD3 34 **What A Fun Day! story**

- Tick if the picture matches the story.
- Cross if the picture doesn't match the story.

3: Concepts lesson

Photocopiable worksheet *Teacher's Book page 205*

CD3 35 CD3 36 **Shining Brightly song**

In the daytime I can hear
Birds singing, birds singing
In the daytime I can see
The sun shining brightly

In the night-time I can hear
Owls hooting, owls hooting
In the night-time I can see
The stars shining brightly

- Point to the pictures and say *daytime* or *night-time*.
- Trace the pictures for *daytime* and *night-time*.
- Draw an extra activity for *daytime* and for *night-time*.
- Match the activities to *daytime* or *night-time*.
- Sing *Shining Brightly* and point to *daytime* and *night-time*.

Dex's values lesson

Bedtime routine

1

8 Discover daily routines

Name: ______________________________

4: Buddy's sounds lesson

Photocopiable worksheet *Teacher's Book page 206*

CD3 37 **Buddy's Beats rap /n/**

1, 2, 3, say with me
/n/, /n/, /n/
/n/ night-time!

1, 2, 3, say with me
/n/, /n/, /n/
/n/ nine!

1, 2, 3, say with me
/n/, /n/, /n/
/n/ noisy!

- Trace the letter /n/.
- Say the sound.
- Point to the pictures and say the words.
- Colour the words beginning with /n/.
- Say *Buddy's Beats* and point to the words beginning with /n/.
- Draw the missing item from *Buddy's Beats*.
- Circle the total number of words beginning with /n/.

5: Dex's values lesson: Bedtime routine

Pupil's Book worksheet *page 97*

- Point to the photos and say the bedtime routine in the correct order.
- Number the photos in the correct order.
- Trace the lines.

1 2 3 ☐ 5 ☐ 7 ☐ 9 ☐

8 Discover daily routines

Name: ______________________________

6: Kid's culture lesson

Pupil's Book worksheet *page 99*

CD3 38 CD3 39 **One, Two, Three, Four, Five nursery rhyme**

One, two, three, four, five
Once I caught a fish alive
Six, seven, eight, nine, ten
Then I let it go again

- Trace and write the numbers one to five.
- Stick the sticker of the fish getting caught on the correct picture.
- Trace and write the numbers six to ten.
- Stick the sticker of the fish escaping on the correct picture.
- Sing *One, Two, Three, Four, Five* and point to the pictures.

7: Speaking and literacy lesson

CD3 34 **Pupils Book worksheet (storybook)** *pages 101–102;*
Photocopiable worksheet *Teacher's Book page 208*

- Cut out and fold the Pupil's Book pages to make the storybook.
- Cut out and fold the Teacher's Book pages to make the cover.
- Listen to the story and follow the storybook with your finger.

8: Review lesson

CD3 42 **Pupil's Book worksheet** *page 103*

- Listen and circle the correct picture.
- Listen again and check your answer.
- Stick Dex's star in the correct place.

Pupil's Book worksheet *page 104*

- Point to the pictures and say the activities.
- Draw a happy/sad face if you can/can't do the activity.

9: PLUS vocabulary lesson / Extension

Photocopiable worksheet *Teacher's Book page 207*

CD3 44 CD3 45 **My Day Is Fun PLUS song**

- Point to and say the activities.
- Trace the frames.
- Number the activities to show the order you do them in, from 1 to 4.
- Colour your favourite activity.
- Sing *My Day Is Fun PLUS*.

2

7

4

5

8
ZZZ

1

6

3

My learning review

1

2

3

My progress review

Name: ______________________

I can …

Teacher: ______________________ Comments: ______________________

Discover Maths

My project 1

Classroom map

My project 1

Classroom map

Discover for yourself

Name: ______________________

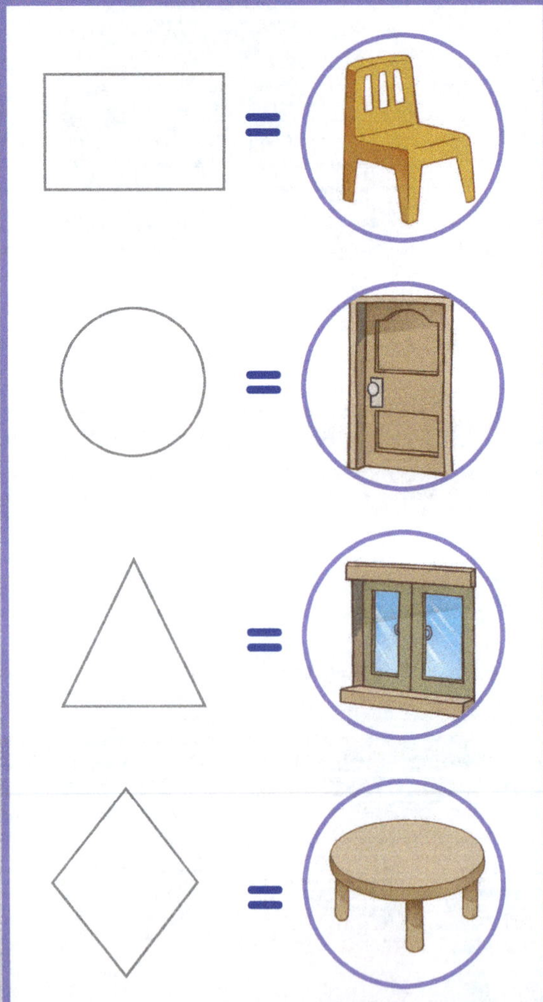

- Colour the key.
- Use the key to draw and colour a map of your classroom.

My project 2

Bones

1

2

3

4

My project 2

Discover Science

Bones

Discover for yourself

Name: ______________________

- Draw bones inside the hand.

My project 3

My home

My home

Discover for yourself

Name: ______________________________

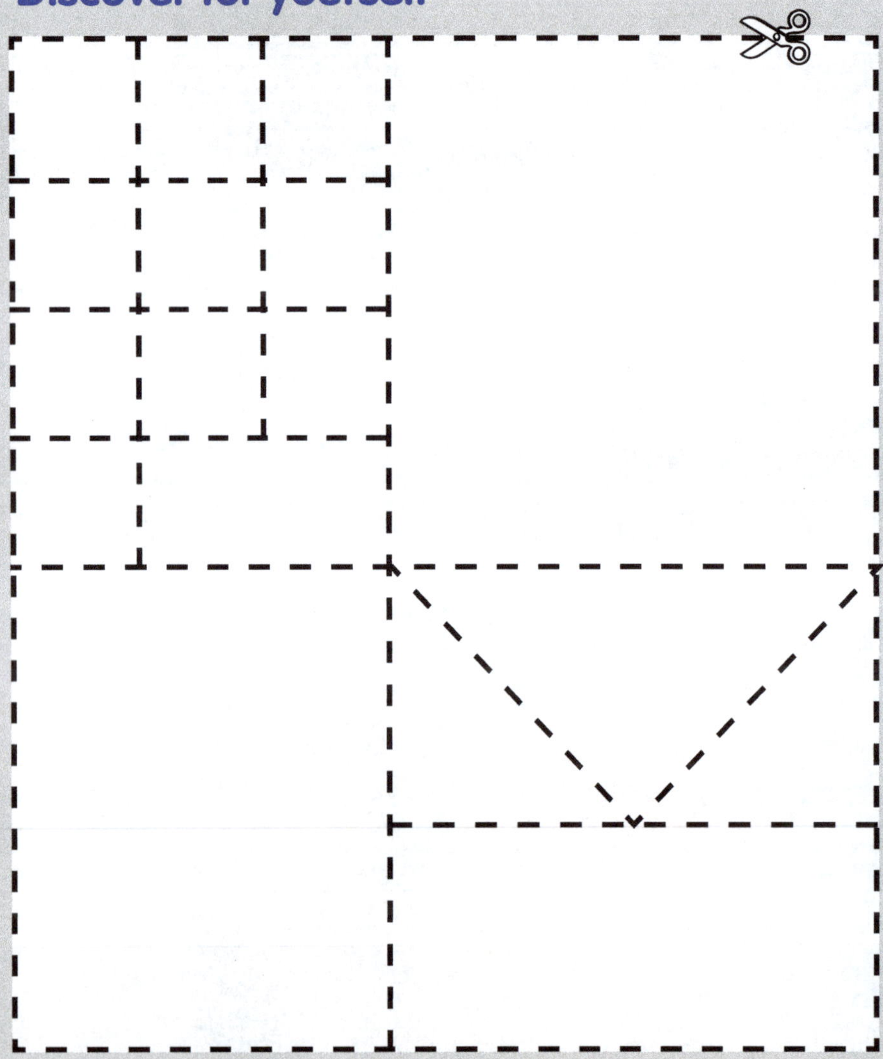

- Cut out the shapes.
- Glue the shapes into the frame to make a house or flat.

Discover Art

My project 4

Camouflage

My project 4

Camouflage

Discover for yourself

Name: ______________________

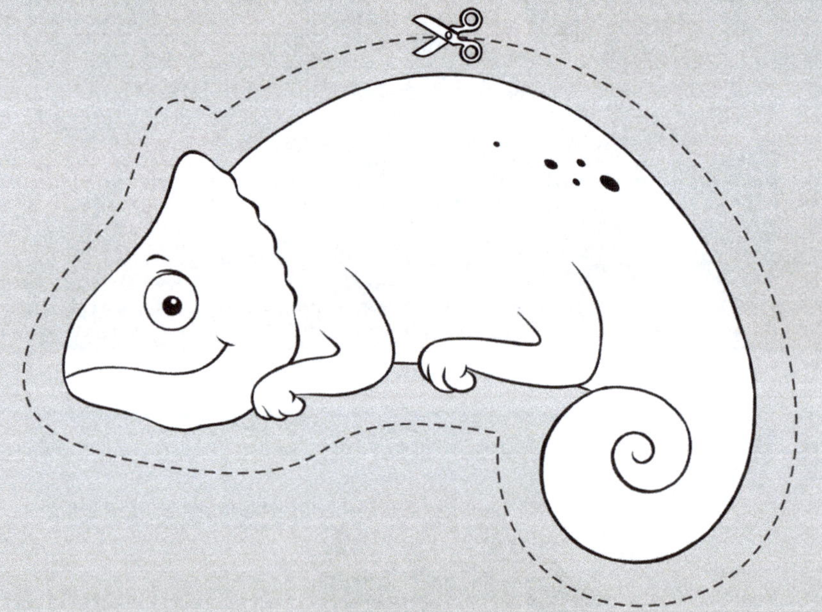

- Colour inside the frame to make a camouflage.
- Colour the chameleon to match.
- Cut out the chameleon and stick it in the frame.

Discover Science

My project 5

Smells

1

2

3

4

My project 5

Discover Science

Smells

Discover for yourself

Name: ____________________

1			✓ ✗
2			✓ ✗
3			✓ ✗

- Smell the containers the teacher gives you. Circle *thumb up* if you like the smell and *thumb down* if you don't.
- Draw what you think the smell is.
- Look at the items the teacher gives you. Circle the tick if you were right and the cross if you were wrong.

Discover Social Science

My project 6

Signs

1

2

3

4

My project 6

Signs

Discover for yourself Name: ______________________

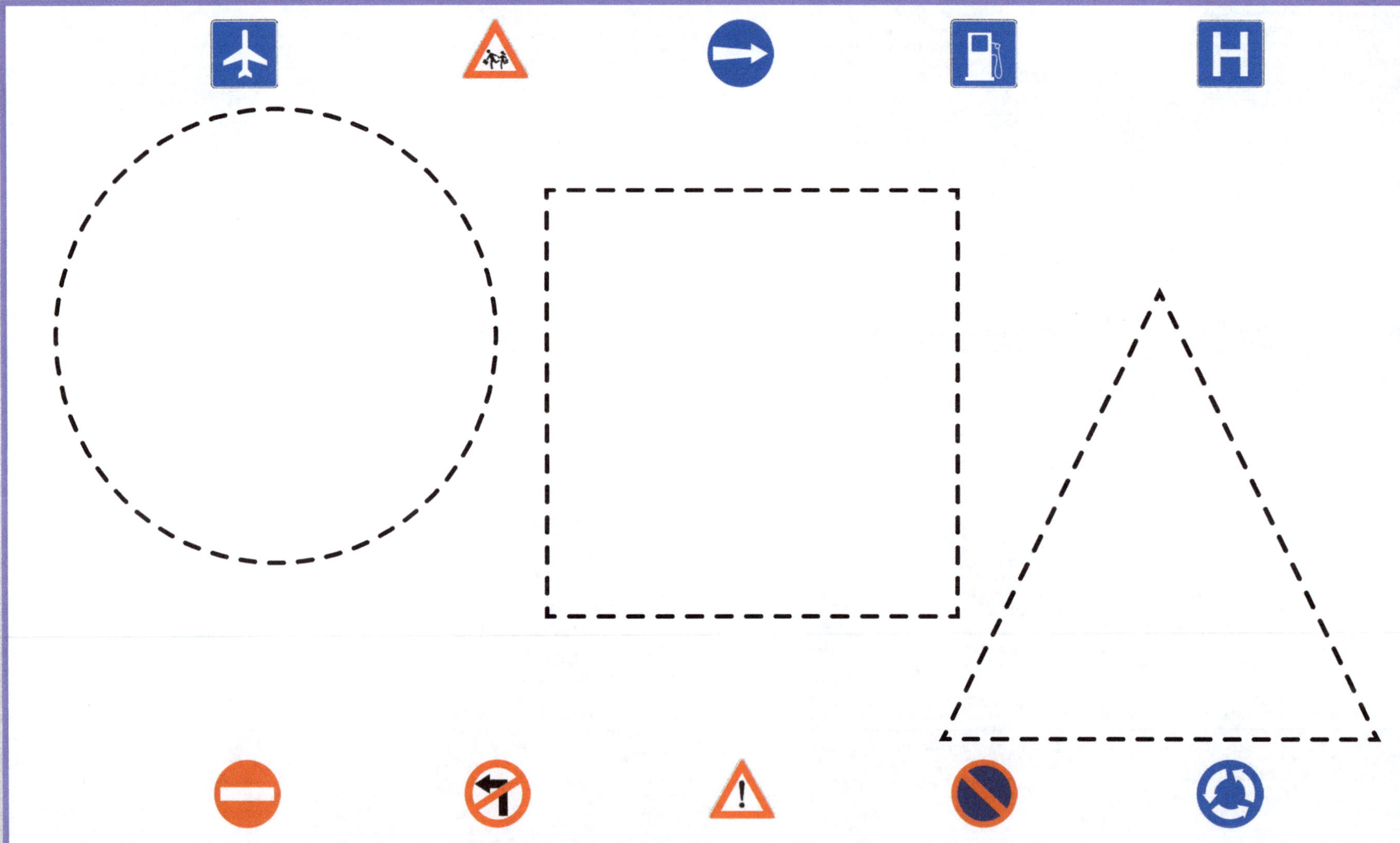

- Trace, draw and colour to make three different road signs.

My project 7

A healthy heart

1

2

3

4

My project 7

A healthy heart

Discover for yourself

Name: ____________________

- Draw an activity that gives you a **slow** heart beat in the top row.
- Draw an activity that gives you a **fast** heart beat in the bottom row.

Healthy eating

My project 8

Healthy eating

Discover for yourself

Name: ______________________

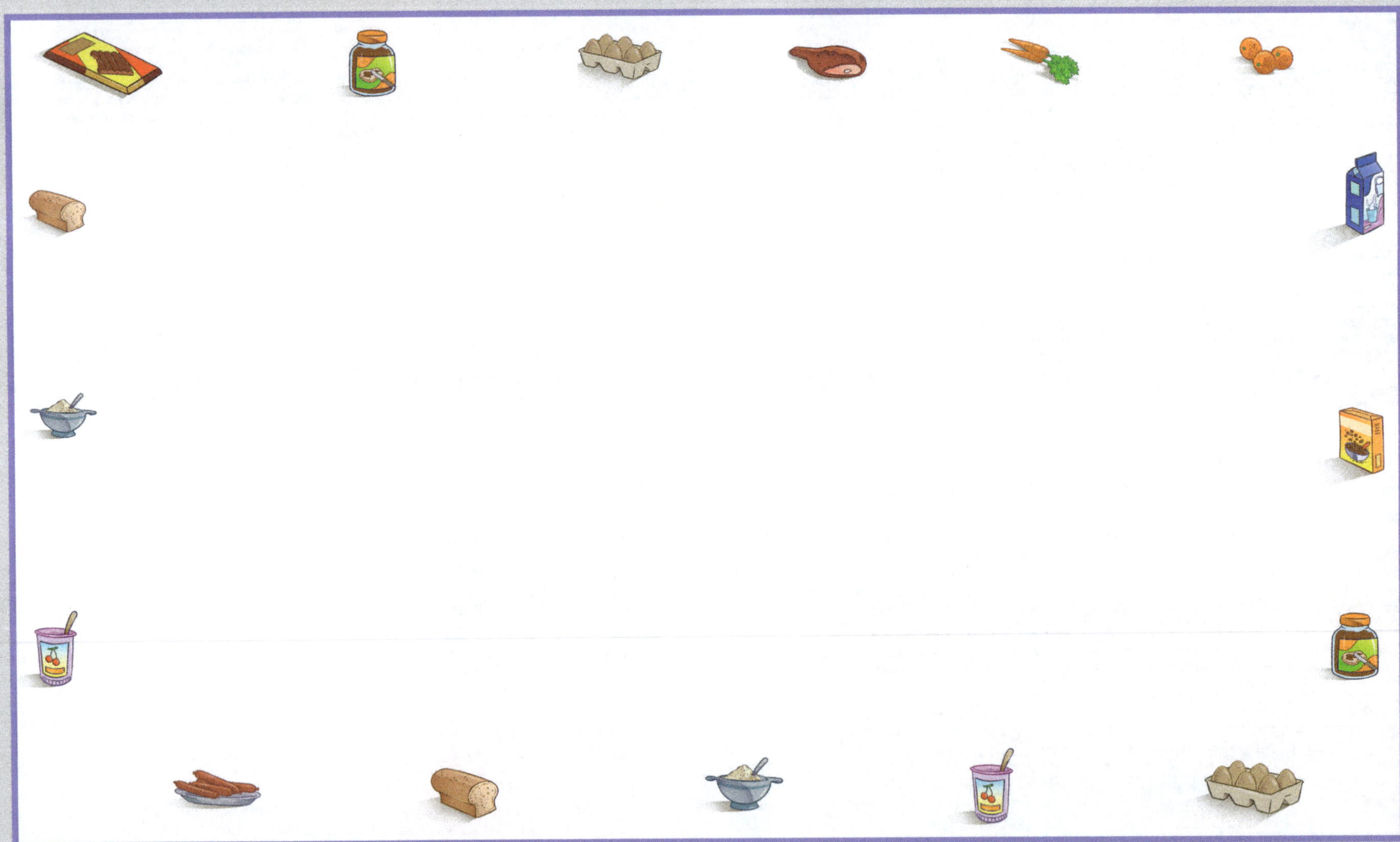

- Draw and colour what you like to eat for breakfast.

Picture dictionary Unit 1

classroom

playground

toilet

dining room

library

gym

PLUS lesson ➔ *Photocopiable worksheet, Teacher's Book page 186*

head teacher

teacher

children

cook

Picture dictionary Unit 2

elbow

knee

head

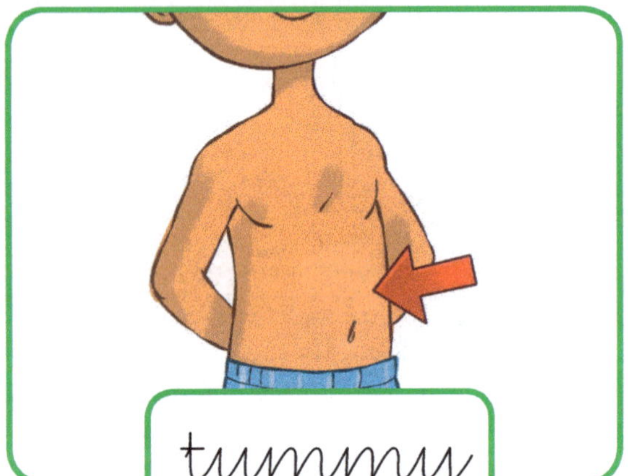
tummy

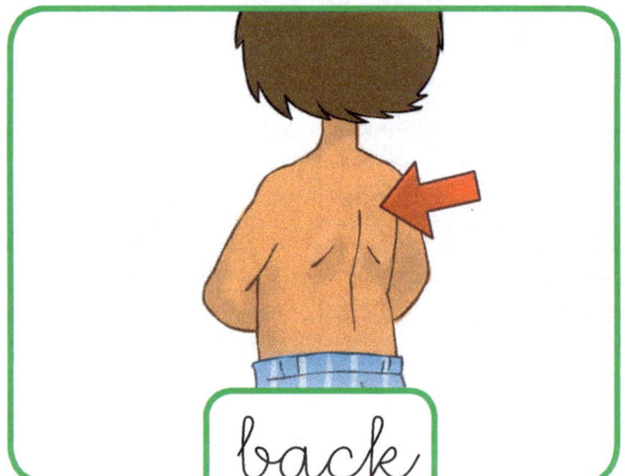
back

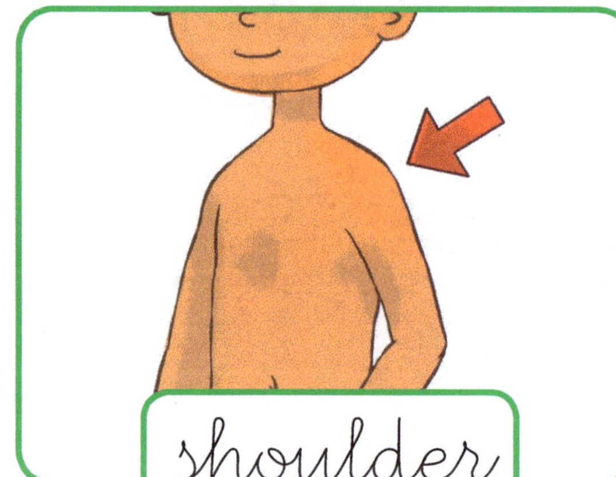
shoulder

PLUS lesson ➡ *Photocopiable worksheet, Teacher's Book page 189*

heart

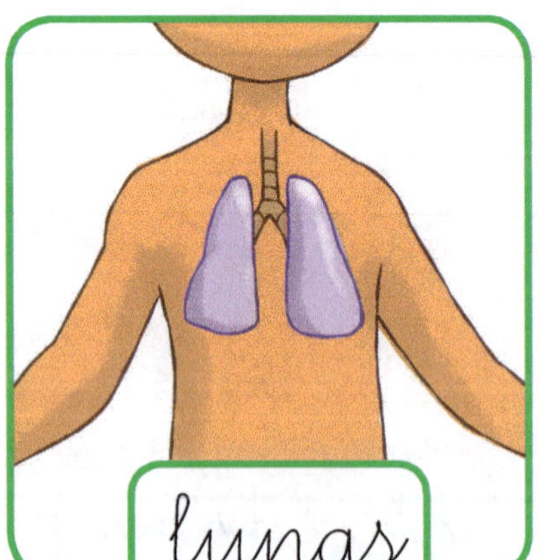
lungs

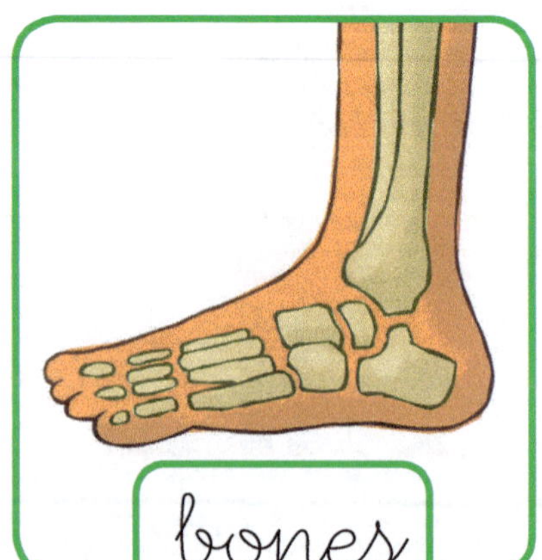
bones

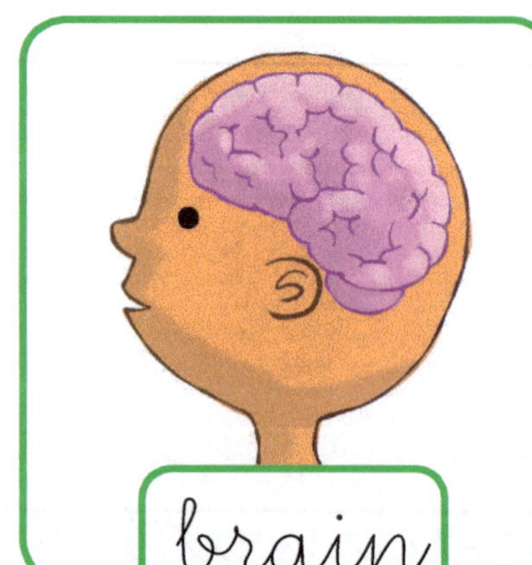
brain

Picture dictionary Unit 3

living room

kitchen

bedroom

garage

garden

bathroom

PLUS lesson ➡ *Photocopiable worksheet, Teacher's Book page 192*

dining room

flat

house

lift

Picture dictionary Unit 4

PLUS lesson ➡ *Photocopiable worksheet, Teacher's Book page 195*

Picture dictionary Unit 5

apple

banana

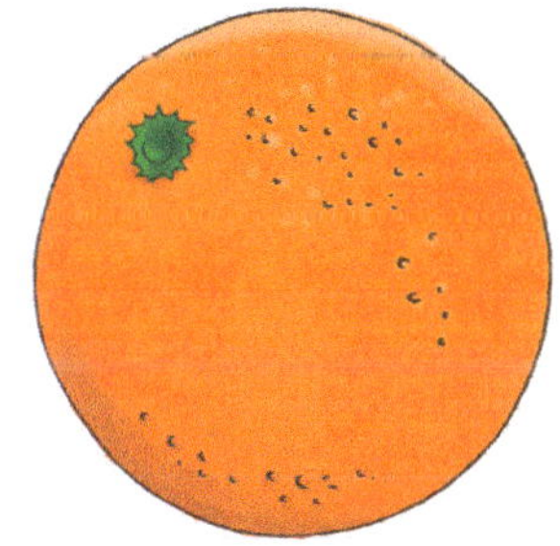

orange

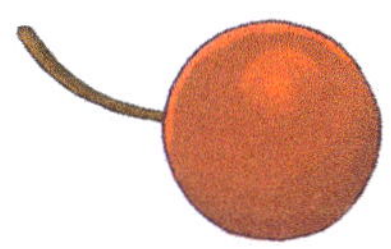

cherry

pear

plum

PLUS lesson ➡ *Photocopiable worksheet, Teacher's Book page 198*

pineapple

strawberry

melon

mango

Picture dictionary Unit 6

police officer

waiter

mechanic

teacher

fire fighter

hairdresser

PLUS lesson ➡ *Photocopiable worksheet, Teacher's Book page 201*

dancer

footballer

vet

shop assistant

Picture dictionary Unit 7

running

skating

playing football

riding a bike

swimming

playing basketball

PLUS lesson ➡ *Photocopiable worksheet, Teacher's Book page 204*

skiing

playing tennis

horse riding

dancing

Picture dictionary Unit 8

get up

get dressed

have breakfast

have dinner

have a bath

go to bed

PLUS lesson ➡ *Photocopiable worksheet, Teacher's Book page 207*

go to school

have a snack

watch TV

play outside

Discover with Dex 2

Unit 1

Unit 2

Unit 3

Unit 4

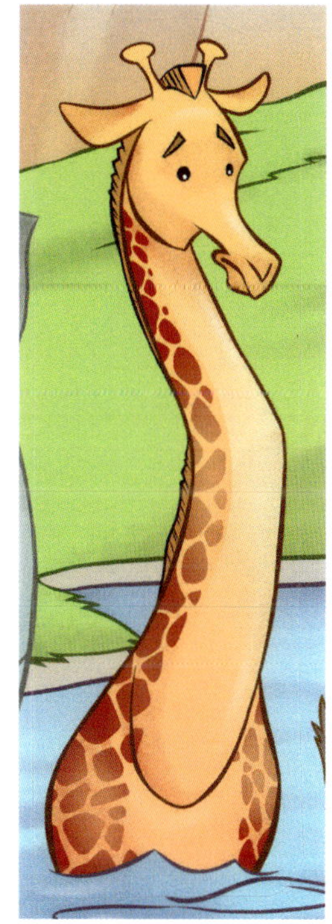

Unit 5

Unit 6

Discover with Dex 2

Unit 7

Unit 8